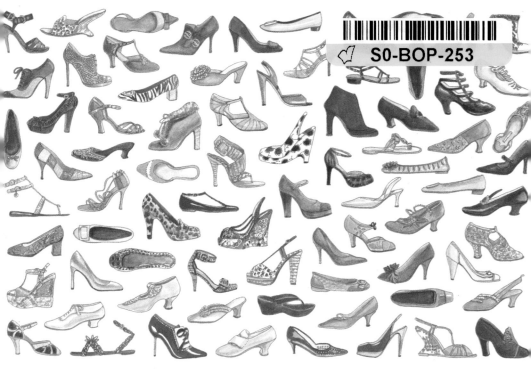

S0-BOP-253

The Five Mile Press Pty Ltd
1 Centre Road, Scoresby
Victoria 3179 Australia
Email: publishing@fivemile.com.au
Website: www.fivemile.com.au

ISBN 978 1 74178 953 9

First published 2008

Printed in China 5 4 3 2

I just love that shoe

ROBYN JOHNSON

ijustlovethat.net

*As responsible publishers
we wouldn't recommend that
anyone with a shoe obsession own
this book, as it may strongly
increase their desire to add to
any existing shoe collection.*

Ballet flats. Peep Toe Shoes, c. 2008.

The heights of fashion.

A collage of a mid-1700s French silk shoe with a 'Louis' heel and paste buckle.

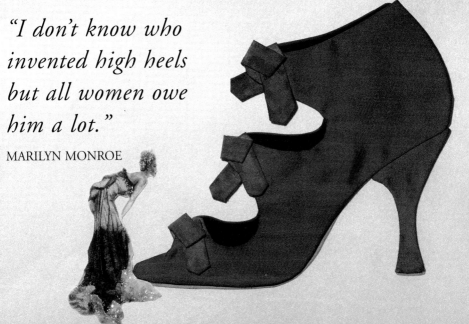

"*I don't know who invented high heels but all women owe him a lot.*"

MARILYN MONROE

A collage of an early 21st century Italian silk shoe with a modernised 'Louis' heel.

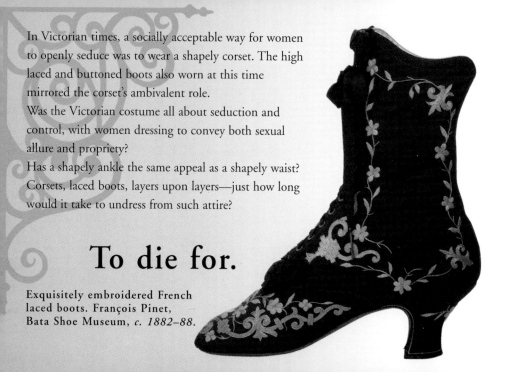

In Victorian times, a socially acceptable way for women to openly seduce was to wear a shapely corset. The high laced and buttoned boots also worn at this time mirrored the corset's ambivalent role.

Was the Victorian costume all about seduction and control, with women dressing to convey both sexual allure and propriety?

Has a shapely ankle the same appeal as a shapely waist?

Corsets, laced boots, layers upon layers—just how long would it take to undress from such attire?

To die for.

Exquisitely embroidered French laced boots. François Pinet, Bata Shoe Museum, *c. 1882–88.*

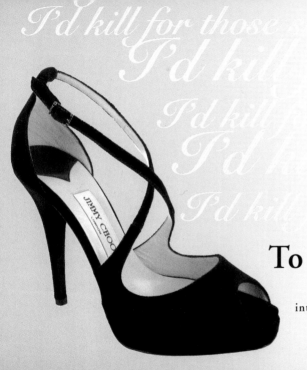

I'd kill for those s...
I'd kill
I'd kill f...
I'd k...
I'd kill

To die for.

No tiptoeing around seductive intentions. Bordeaux velvet platform shoe. Jimmy Choo, *c. 2007*.

A collage of a shoe designed by Pietro Yanturni in the 1920s.

The most expensive shoemaker in the world.

Imagine if you could afford to employ a gifted shoemaker to custom-make all of your shoes, fitting like pairs of silk socks and fashioned from materials such as antique laces and velvets. In the early 1900s, Rita de Acosta Lydig commissioned Pietro Yanturni, the East Indian curator of shoes at the Cluny Museum in Paris, to do just that. Yanturni's exclusive clientele had moulds made for each foot that resulted in incredibly light, sculpted footwear. A deposit of one thousand dollars secured delivery in two to three years. (But can you imagine waiting that long?)

"A shoe without sex appeal is as barren as a tree without leaves." RITA DE ACOSTA LYDIG

$\mathcal{W}$ith a history beginning in 1851, Bally has continued to make beautiful shoes of style and comfort. Their tradition for making such elegant and well-crafted shoes has continued through to the present day. Have you ever been seduced by superb workmanship and quality to the point that you will no longer accept less because you understand the true value of a beautiful shoe? Do you believe that if you are wearing the right shoes, the rest is mere detail?

An illustration influenced by the fashions of Paul Poiret from the early 1900s.

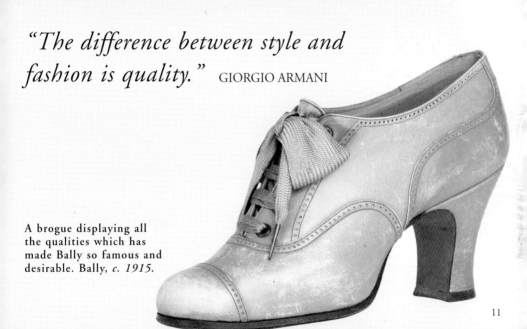

"The difference between style and fashion is quality." GIORGIO ARMANI

A brogue displaying all the qualities which has made Bally so famous and desirable. Bally, *c. 1915*.

11

"Style is primarily a matter of instinct." BILL BLASS

The 1920s era was a celebration of youth and life, full of parties and sport.

A thriving art scene influenced life and design, and a passion for jazz took hold as fashionable flappers danced the nights away.

What style of shoe would any free-spirited girl wear to keep up? Those with a t-bar or ankle strap, of course.

Gold and multi-coloured textile bar shoe with a 'Louis' heel. Dutch, Bata Shoe Museum, *c. 1922–25*.

Right: A classic Bally shoe design from 1937 that has been reinterpreted in recent collections. Bally, *c. 2007*.

Opposite: A striking shoe reminiscent of the jazz era. Peep Toe Shoes, *c. 2007*.

13

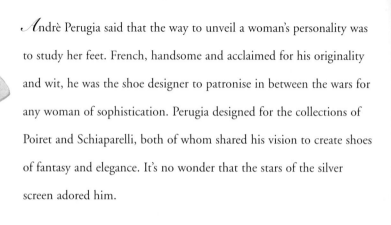

*A*ndrè Perugia said that the way to unveil a woman's personality was to study her feet. French, handsome and acclaimed for his originality and wit, he was the shoe designer to patronise in between the wars for any woman of sophistication. Perugia designed for the collections of Poiret and Schiaparelli, both of whom shared his vision to create shoes of fantasy and elegance. It's no wonder that the stars of the silver screen adored him.

"Dreams are necessary to life."

ANAÏS NIN

A collage inspired by Perugia's 1931 fish-shaped needle-heeled stiletto made for Jourdan of France.

High-heeled pumps with 'Aladdin' toe designed by Perugia for Schiaparelli's Circus Collection, Bata Shoe Museum, *c. 1937–38.*

Vintage modern.

Salvatore Ferragamo took the world to new heights with his imaginative designs. He was a resourceful designer who constantly created modern shoes that pushed the boundaries of shoe design, many becoming icons in their own right.

An illustration of a 1938 platform and heel in cork layers covered in rainbow-coloured suede by Salvatore Ferragamo.

Vintage.

Glam-rock gold and turquoise
platform mules said to have
been designed for Biba.
Bata Shoe Museum, *c. 1972–75.*

Modern.

Platform sandal in
gold metallic leather
with striking gold heel.
Dior, *c. 2007.*

"Change is the healthiest way to survive."
KARL LAGERFELD

A collage inspired by
Salvatore Ferragamo's
witty 1935 raffia sandal
that used corks to
form the heel.

18

Ferragamo's innovative use of materials, due to wartime rationing, still has influence today. The talented designer's inspiring determination to cut through the mainstream has paved the way for others to pursue the unexpected. And with the current increase in demand for the sustainable use of materials, Ferragamo's designs will no doubt continue to inspire.

Handmade pumps covered in vintage Japanese kimono fabric designed with style and sustainability in mind. Hetty Rose, *c. 2007.*

Wedge-heeled sandal with straw detailing pays homage to Ferragamo's original designs of 1936. Nine West, *c. 2007–08.*

Large brogue with punching, pleating and stitching detail, with a ballet-point toe. Preston Zly, *c. 2005.*

A contemporary bootie displaying the influence of Ferragamo's ankle boots of the 1930s. Dior, *c. 2007.*

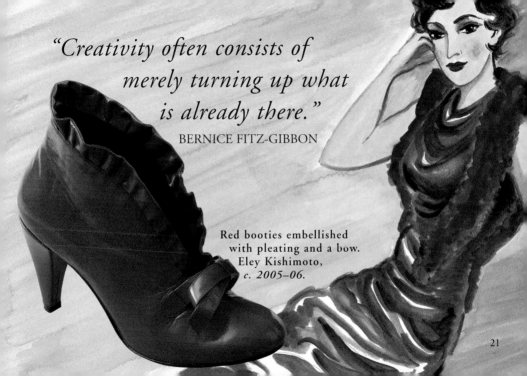

> *"Creativity often consists of merely turning up what is already there."*
>
> BERNICE FITZ-GIBBON

Red booties embellished
with pleating and a bow.
Eley Kishimoto,
c. 2005–06.

"Fashion fades, only style remains the same."

COCO CHANEL

*I*n the late 1930s, the open toe and sling back were

introduced, but it wasn't until the 1940s when

stockings without reinforced toes and heels were

manufactured that the styles became popular.

A classic Bally shoe design
with a handmade flower from
1947 has been reinterpreted
in recent collections.
Bally, *c. 2007.*

> *"Fashion is architecture.*
> *It is a matter of proportions."*
>
> COCO CHANEL

*M*any shoe designers worked on developing a shoe with a slim and elegant heel, but Roger Vivier tends to be credited for developing the stiletto. When Dior launched his 'New Look' in 1947, Roger Vivier teamed up with him to create shoes to go with this softer silhouette, borrowing techniques employed in towering architecture and aeronautics to develop the stiletto's needle-like heel.

24

Seduced by design?

Features that have become
the 'classic' stiletto: black in
colour, needle-like high-heel
and pointy toe.
Salvatore Ferragamo,
Bata Shoe Museum,
c. 1955.

> ## "Who ever said that pleasure wasn't functional?"
> CHARLES EAMES

$\mathcal{B}$allet flats, low sling backs and pumps came into their own once Audrey Hepburn, Brigitte Bardot and Jean Seberg began wearing them in their movies.

There is a fresh, demure and girlish sexiness to those who freely get about in a simple pair of flats, especially when teamed with sporty capri pants and a knotted white shirt or simple LBD.

These have become classic shoe styles thanks to functionality and their association with some of the world's most stylish women.

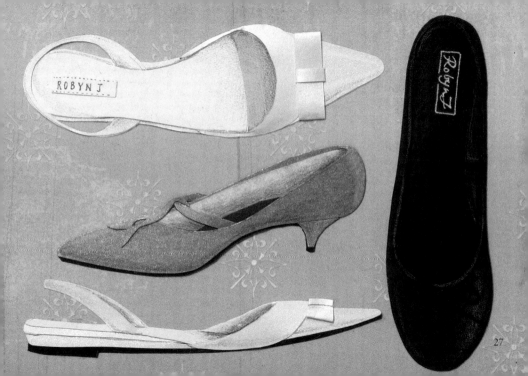

27

> *"I always considered the shoe as an object, like a piece of sculpture."*
>
> ROGER VIVIER

Roger Vivier was yet another brilliant shoe designer worthy of any shoe lover's attention. Known as the Fabergé of shoes for creating footwear that brilliantly set off the clothes that they were paired with, Vivier designed shoes for the coronation of Queen Elizabeth II, and many of the world's fashionable figures from Marlene Dietrich to Jackie O.

Collages inspired by some of Vivier's masterful designs.

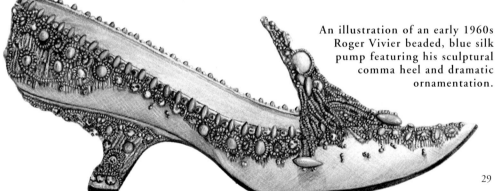

An illustration of an early 1960s Roger Vivier beaded, blue silk pump featuring his sculptural comma heel and dramatic ornamentation.

It's a jungle out there.

"My weakness is wearing too much leopard print."

JACKIE COLLINS

*F*orget anything primitive like walking through concrete jungles in great heels embellished with animal skin, they're far better suited to dangling off the toes of A-listers seated in the front row of a fashion show.

This page: Leopard-skin print stiletto. Jimmy Choo, *c. 2007*.

Opposite: Various ways to skin a shoe by Dior, Sergio Rossi and Jimmy Choo, *c. 2007*.

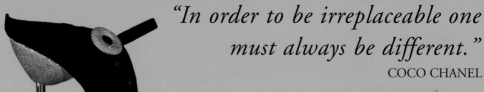

> *"In order to be irreplaceable one must always be different."*
>
> COCO CHANEL

Shoes are a girl's best friend! Especially when they are encrusted with 3,500 diamonds. Preston Zly for Holloway Diamonds valued at A$155,000, *c. 2007.*

Peep-toe ankle-strap shoe with innovative heel. Jimmy Choo, *c. 2007.*

*B*eth Levine reportedly had dreams at night of making shoes. She created one daring design after another for the shoe company that she set up with her husband, Herbert, in the late 1940s. Her creatively inspiring and trend-setting designs opened up a whole world of possibilities for the continuing creation of original shoes.

Blue velvet mule with innovative silver-rolled leather heel. Beth Levine, Bata Shoe Museum, *c. 1954.*

> *"There is no limit to beauty, no saturation point in design."*
>
> SALVATORE FERRAGAMO

New materials and youth culture inspired much of the shoe design of the Sixties. Street style and ready-to-wear generally set the trends rather than a handful of couture establishments.

A collage inspired by Roger Vivier's pilgrim pump with its silver buckle. Designed for Catherine Deneuve in the 1967 film *Belle de Jour*, it is often cited as the most copied shoe of all time.

The space age was embraced on the dance floor and on the street. A collage inspired by Courrèges' 1964 futuristic go-go boot.

These boots are made for ...

It has been said that we can thank the riding boot for the development of the heel—a much-needed feature added to prevent the foot from slipping in stirrups. The beloved boot has always had an important role to play, be it for assertion, magic, eroticism or simply fashion.

Boots featured by Jimmy Choo, Dior and Sergio Rossi,
c. 2007.

every Nancy,

Puss and Barbarella.

"You put high heels on and you change."

MANOLO BLAHNIK

All the better to boogie in; go on, strut your stuff.

It is a known fact that, on average, a woman's derriere protrudes 25% more when she wears high heels.

Gold lamé and leather platform sandal. Sergio Rossi, *c. 2007.*

Silver strapped and gold plastic platform sandals. Scardavi Benito, Bata Shoe Museum, *c. 1976–79.*

Opposite: A collage inspired by 1940s rhinestone-studded platforms designed for Hollywood divas, a glamorous design that has constantly been revived.

39

Shoe candy: sweet, addictive and without the calories. Featuring shoes by Peep Toe Shoes, Sergio Rossi, Nine West and Dior, *c. 2007*.

I want candy.

David Evins, who designed the shoes Grace Kelly
wore when she married Prince Rainier,
was adored by many celebrities
and the fashion elite for
his ability to design
shoes that embodied
who they were.

A collage inspired by a multicoloured 1934 pave wedge designed by David Evins.

"My shoes are special shoes for discerning feet."
MANOLO BLAHNIK

*O*nce upon a time, there was a magical shoe designer who

completely and utterly understood how to make women sigh,

mastered 'shoe cleavage', and tapped the potent sexuality

of a beautiful shoe.

Actually he is very real … this masterful designer's name is

Manolo Blahnik, and he is the king of 'limousine shoes'.

**Opposite: A collage celebrating shoes of whimsy
and delightful impracticality.**

43

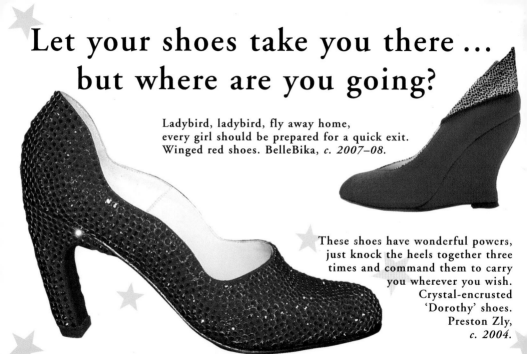

Let your shoes take you there ...
but where are you going?

Ladybird, ladybird, fly away home,
every girl should be prepared for a quick exit.
Winged red shoes. BelleBika, *c. 2007–08.*

These shoes have wonderful powers,
just knock the heels together three
times and command them to carry
you wherever you wish.
Crystal-encrusted
'Dorothy' shoes.
Preston Zly,
c. 2004.

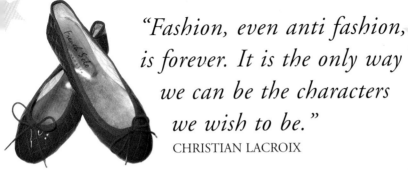

> *"Fashion, even anti fashion, is forever. It is the only way we can be the characters we wish to be."*
> CHRISTIAN LACROIX

But beware of being seduced by red slippers, there's no telling where they might take you. Quilted patent red ballet flats. London Sole, *c. 2007*.

Every girl should own a pair of shoes that wouldn't ever be worn anywhere practical, but could always take her anywhere that her heart desires. Red leather heels wrapped with sweet cherry fabric. Sergio Rossi, *c. 2007*.

45

Photographic images kindly supplied by the following designers and establishments:

Bally: 11, 13 (right), 22.

Bata Shoe Museum, Toronto: 6, 13 (left), 15, 17 (left), 25, 33, 39 (right), 43. (All images © 2008 Bata Shoe Museum, Toronto.)

BelleBika: 44 (right).

Dior: 17 (right), 20 (right), 30, 36, 40.

Eley Kishimoto: 21.

Getty Images: 23.

Hetty Rose: 19 (right).

Jacqui Henshaw: Photography of all collages.

Also available in this exquisitely
packaged accessories trio:

'I just love that bag'
'I just love that hat'

10 themed gift cards with envelopes
accompany each 48-page book.

ROBYN JOHNSON

Do you want more?

ijustlovethat.net

A website with links to designers,
museums and vintage sellers
and with information on where to buy
I just love that...'
publications and stationery.